Spirit of Fredericksburg

An artist's view of a historic town.

Art by Tanya Richey
Written by April Bair

Thanks to all the friends, family & patrons who keep Tanya's spirit alive through her art.

Introduction

Tanya Richey, a Virginia native, worked to capture the spirit of Fredericksburg. Her vision for this book was to take readers along on a visual tour of the Fredericksburg she knew and loved.

Painting was her way to communicate with the world around her, letting people see through her eyes. These paintings show Fredericksburg as Richey experienced it from the 1980s-2018.

Spirit of Fredericksburg is a narrative collection of art, history, and contemporary life. Moments of visiting, living, and working in "the Burg" captured by her brushstrokes.

This book presents part of a collection of original paintings depicting her interpretation of Fredericksburg and its history. along side stories and anecdotal information from years of local conversation. Guests from near and far came into the *Tanya Richey Studio Gallery* at 817 Caroline street sharing their take on things. Those stories are presented by her daughter and gallery business partner April Bair.

Spirit of Fredericksburg:
An Artist's View of a historical town.

First edition. December 2019. Bair Ink.

Fredericksburg, Virginia, USA.

ALL RIGHTS RESERVED
ISBN-13: 978-1-7329042-5-5
LCCN: 2019950048

Artwork © Tanya M. Richey
Written by April Bair
FXBG font created by Nick Curtus

Adapted from a 2013 Fredericksburg Art Exhibition for Cultural Exchange partner city program between Fredericksburg, Virginia & Schwetzingen, Germany.

No portion of this book may be reproduced for other than review purposes without prior written consent.

www.BairInk.com

Tanya M Richey

Spirit of Fredericksburg
An artist's view of a historic town

Art by Tanya Richey

Written by April Bair

Fredericksburg, Virginia

Table of Contents

A Story of Fredericksburg, Virginia
    The Fredericksburg Painting 8
    Fredericksburg Painting in Spring 9

Local Tribes
    Patawomeck fisherman 12

Mary Ball Washington 14
    Mary Ball's House at Epping Forest 16
    The Mary Washington House in Fredericksburg 17

George Washington
    Popes Creek, Washington's Birthplace 18
    Crossing the Rappahannock to Ferry Farm 19
    Washington's Women at Kenmore 20
    Colonial Independence Day 21

Portraits of Past and Present
    Olde Fredericksburg Dock 22
    Olde Mill District 23
    Rising Sun Tavern 24
    Hugh Mercer Apothecary 25
    Kenmore House 26
    Kenmore Inn 27
    Fredericksburg Fires 28
    The Wells House 29
    The Old Stone Warehouse 30
    Virginia Tobaco Jar 31
    Back of Old Town Hall 32
    Princess Anne Street 33
    Fredericksburg Square 34
    509 Caroline Street 35
    The Circuit Court House 36
    Irish Eyes 38
    Olde Silk Mill 40
    400 Hanover Street 41
    St George's Church at Night 42
    Fredericksburg United Methodist Church 43
    Shiloh Baptist Church & Walker-Grant School 45
    Tea at Smythe Cottage 46
    Tru Luv's Patio 47
    Carl's Ice Cream 48
    Castiglia's on William Street 49

    Art Comes Alive 50
    Impressions of Caroline Street 51
    Gari Melcher's Belmont 52

Theatre and the Arts
    Girls of the Golden Afternoon 53

Fredericksburg Gateway to the World
    Fredericksburg Dinner Cruise in Spring 54
    Antique Cars Show on Caroline Street 55
    Riverboat on the Rappahannock 56

Behind the Train Station 58
    Pufferbellies 60
    The William Street Bridge 61

Animals and Agriculture
    Dogs Welcome 62
    Dogs on Caroline Street 63

The Chicken Controversy
    Rooster and His Hen House 64
    Rubaiyat of Omar Khayyam Chicken 65
    The Fredericksburg Fair 66
    Virgina Cows 67
    Summer Barn 68
    Weathervane Barn 69
    Virgina Wild Turkey 70

Wild Life
    The Rocky Fall Line 71
    Rappahannock Winter 72

Afterword 73

Resources 74

Index 75

Author Bio 77

A Story of Fredericksburg, Virginia

Relic hunters enjoy searching local woods for Revolutionary and Civil War relics like lead bullets and belt buckles, but local history runs much deeper. Archaeologists have found evidence of much older inhabitants. Excavation reveals tools of prehistoric hunter-gatherer people as far back as 10,000 BC and Woodland Indian artifacts from 1,500BC.

In 1728 Fredericksburg was formally established by charter from the House of Burgesses. By that time the little 'burg and neighboring village, Falmouth, already hosted homes with established trade.

Cpt. John Smith mapped the Falmouth area in 1608 on an expedition west, John Lederer surveyed what would become known as Fredericksburg in 1670, and in 1671 Sir William Berkelay executed a deed of Sovereignty to

> The first legal record of the place as a community is had in 1671... forty colonists established what is now the heart of Fredericksburg, but known in those remote times as 'Leaseland.'– John T. Goolrick.

Thomas Royston and John Buckner

With the Royston-Buckner Plan, which laid out the streets, the official name became Fredericksburg for Prince Frederick Louis of Hanover. (Son of King George II and the Prince of Wales). The streets were named after royal family members including Sophia of Hanover and Caroline of Ansbach.

In 1777 the emerging city was already a center of political action and the Virgina Statute of Religious Liberty was drafted here.

Colonial Fredericksburg was constructed mainly of wooden buildings within a few blocks of the river. Then, Allentown and Libertytown neighborhoods were drawn up and the village grew into the modern day city limits.

Today, Fredericksburg is an blend of history, subdivisions, shopping malls, and luxury apartments

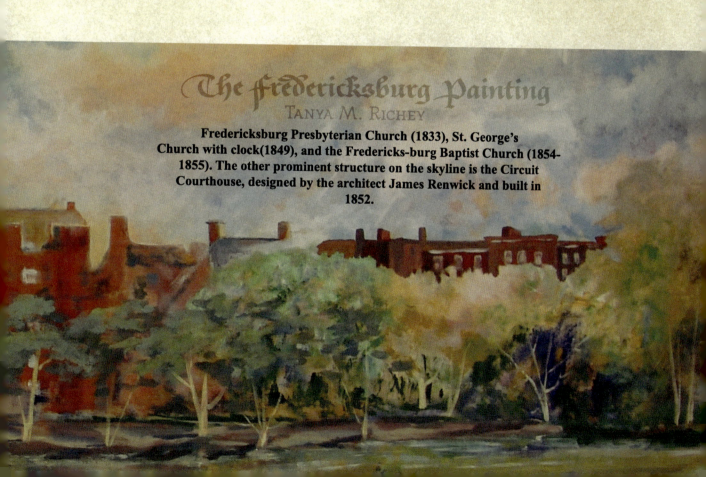

The Fredericksburg Painting
Tanya M. Richey

Fredericksburg Presbyterian Church (1833), St. George's Church with clock(1849), and the Fredericks-burg Baptist Church (1854-1855). The other prominent structure on the skyline is the Circuit Courthouse, designed by the architect James Renwick and built in 1852.

alongside preserved buildings and establishments of bygone eras but, the basic footprint of downtown Fredericksburg remains.

Revolutionary War Era buildings still stand including the Hugh Mercer Apothecary, Rising Sun Tavern, and Kenmore Mansion holding history of America's birth.

The Fredericksburg skyline has not changed much since the 1800s. Tanya Richey's iconic Fredericksburg painting features three steeples visible since the 1800s. The bridge she depicted, Scott's bridge, was destroyed by Confederate forces during the Civil War and replaced by the Chatham Bridge which was rebuilt in the 1930s with extensive renovated in 2020. Further upriver, in Falmouth, was a toll bridge crossing the Rappahannock River so during the 1900s Chatham bridge became known as the free bridge.

Fredericksburg has a rich history of factories dating back to the 1700s when mills feed by river power processed silk, wool, wood, grist, and sumac. The mill area (seen in the right side of the painting) was full of the most modern technology. The area welcomed the Rappahannock Electric Light and

Power Company in 1887 and dams were built to control the fierce Rappahannock.

Following the river downstream are the train bridge (1926) and the city dock (not shown in the painting). During Fredericksburg seaport days the banks were lined with wharfs. Schooners and other great ships brought trade from as far away as the West Indies, England, Spain

The paintings on this and the previous page depicts a loose perspective looking down from the hill at Chatham Manor on the Stafford side of the river. While pruning rose bushes at Chatham, the artist looked across the river toward Fredericksburg imagining the view throughout history. The original townscape was painted on a 4' by 6' birch wood board and depicts Fredericksburg through the ages.

THE ORIGINAL TOWNSCAPE PAINTING OF RIVERSIDE FREDERICKSBURG, often called Tanya Richey's *Fredericksburg Painting*, is pictured on the previous page in it's original colors. From that painting prints were made which she altered to created visions of Fredericksburg is various seasons such as Spring Fredericksburg seen here. The original painting includes a scene of local fisherman smoking Shad fish in the right corner which can be seen on page 13.

Local Tribes

Before European settlers arrived, native peoples controlled the area. Powhatan, Doegg, Sesquehannock, Seneca, Piscataways and even Iriquous hunted the woods. Patawomeck and Manahoacks tribes thrived. The wooded land provided an ample supply of wildlife sustained by two major rivers. Fresh water routes, natural resources and mild climate made the region a natural thoroughfare for indigenous peoples beckoning inter-tribe trade.

Local woodland Indians were divided at the fall line of the Rappahannock River with Manahoac tribes upriver from the fall line break (Falmouth). The Patawomeck centered between the Rappahannock and Potomac Rivers.

European explorers were not welcomed and violent skirmishes broke out with Captain John Smith and the Manahoac.

The Manahoac died out and their territory, Spotsylvania, became settled by Alexander Spotswood who brought in a German settlement to for iron works, Germanna.

The Patawomeck were an agricultural trading society, an independent tribe of the Powhatan Chieftain, one of eleven recognized Native American tribes in Virginia. localized in the White Oak area.

Trade formed but the relationship between settlers and Indians was wrought with changing alliances.

Captain John Smith documented his time with the Patawomeck tribe including detailed notes on culture and their Algonquian

SKETCH OF PATAWOMECK
Tribe member and canoe completed as part of Fredericksburg Painting preparation.

> "Some of the names mentioned by Captain John Smith have been in constant use from his day with but slight change in spelling. Nearly all of these belong to the Powhatan language. -William Wallace Tooker 1901.

language but after the English declared war in 1666 the tribe disappeared from all records. Indians and settlers married blending the cultures together and despite many prominent local families of tribal decent the Patawomeck were historically inviable until the 20th century. Virginia State recognition came in 2010 when tribal member and celebrity Wayne Newton testified to the Virgina House and Senate.

The modern Patawomeck work to revive their lost language and envision their native language taught in Stafford County Public Schools.

Heritage unites the tribe of Proud People but so much of their culture and customs were lost leaving only foreign records and legends such as details regarding the kidnapping and of Pocahontas kidnapped from a Patawomeck village on the banks of the Potomac in modern day Stafford County.

The iconic townscape of Fredericksburg painted by Tanya Richey pays homage to local Native American history. A traditional Patawomeck structure is depicted in the foreground along with fishermen smoking their catch. These fish, Shad, still swim the Rappahannock River but today's fish are much smaller.

Industrialization and dam building disturbed the migration runs but in spring Blue Heron are still plentiful on river rocks near the Falmouth Bridge feeding on the silvery fish. It's said that the Shad pulled from the river used to be as long as a boy is tall.

PATAWOMECK FISHING FOR SHAD.
Cropped from Richey's Fredericksburg Painting.

Most reproductions of the original painting do not include the Patawomeck fishermen in the bottom right corner because the most popular reproduction size was a 12" x 36" rectangular prints which required that section of the painting be cropped out.

PORTRAIT OF MARY BALL WASHINGTON.
**Acrylic mural on board.
Rendered based on primary source descriptions of George Washington's mother.**

Mary Ball Washington

George Washington's mother might be the soul of Fredericksburg still praying from Meditation Rock. The hospital, university, and local Womans Club are named after her, and her home on Charles Street draws daily visitors

Artist Tanya Richey was surprised to discover that despite Mary's honored place in American history and undeniable influence on Fredericksburg there were are few renderings her. Mary Ball Washington never sat for a portrait (which was not uncommon for women of the day).

In 2012 Richey was commissioned by the owners of local restaurant, *The Virginia Deli*, to paint a mural to hide functional but unsightly aspects of the restaurant's building. America's mother became the subject.

(The deli was later moved from Sophia Street to Caroline Street and closed in 2018.)

Since no lifetime portraits of Mary exist Richey researched by reading diary entries and historic letters from the era. Correspondence between friends, family, and neighbors describe her looks and demeanor. Richey also worked from portraits of George Washington and other family members, including Mary's father, to imagine what Mary Washington looked like later in life when she lived in Fredericksburg.

Richey's portrait came together as a mounted mural painted in acrylic on board. Originally, the portrait hung on Sophia street facing the Chatham Bridge as a welcoming visitors into Fredericksburg.

In 2014 the portrait was loaned to the Mary Ball Washington Museum and Library in Lancaster, Virginia.

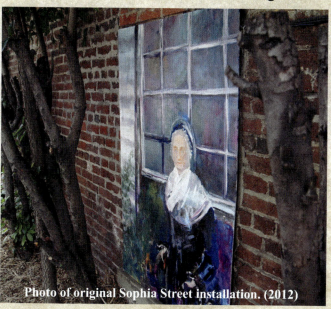
Photo of original Sophia Street installation. (2012)

Mary Ball's House at Epping Forest

Mary Ball, George Washington's mother, was born in Lively, Virginia around 1708.

Epping Forest is the birthplace of Mary Ball Washing. It was her father's plantation in Lively, Virginia where she lived as a young child. The original plantation house has been lost over the years, but this private residence stands where Mary Ball once lived.

Eping Forest Portrai
Watervcolor on paper.

Her father, William Ball, died when Mary was three and she moved, with her mother, to Cherry Point on the Potomac until her mother died and George Eskridge became her guardian.

In 1731 at the age of 22 she married Virginia planter Augustine Washington and moved to his plantation in the Northern Neck. They had five children before Augustine died (George Washington's was 16). Before Augustine's death the family moved from Popes Creek Plantation to Ferry Farm which Mary enjoyed.

Mary Washington loved and respected her son however, many believe they differed on political issues. According to some sources most of the family supported rebellion, but Mary Ball Washington was loyal to England. It's rumored that after the Revolutionary War she wore black mourning not only the lives lost but also, the Colonial split from England.

As the Revolutionary War

The Mary Washington House in Fredericksburg

Mary Ball Washington lived in Fredericksburg until her death in 1789.

Mary Washington House in Winter
Watercolor on paper.

approached George wanted his mother to move into the safety of town and in 1772 he purchased a house at the intersection of Charles and Lewis streets for £225.

In 1774 Mary reluctantly agreed to move across the river into the town house. Mary was a headstrong independent widow, who'd run a profitable farm as a single mother. She was hesitant to leave her plantation but eventually George's growing concern about the forthcoming war won out.

Living in Fredericksburg she had a front seat to America's birth at a crossroads of emerging pivotal leaders. Mother Washington hosted many notable visitors in the comfortable house including George Mason and Marquis de Lafayette (who adored her gingerbread) but, she's recorded saying the only pleasant thing about living in town was being able to walk to church.

George Washington
Popes Creek, Washington's Birthplace

Portrait of Popes Creek
Watercolor on paper painted on site.

George Washington's grandfather settled Popes Creek Plantation in 1657 after being shipwrecked nearby. The tobacco growing property sits between the tributary at Popes Creek and the Potomac River. During the 17th and 18th century the waterway was a main shipping route to the Atlantic Ocean.

George Washington was born at Popes Creek in 1718 and lived there until age 6 when the family moved to Stafford County bank of the Rappahannock River. Today, Popes Creek is owned by the National Park Service preserving the atmosphere with a memorial house and grounds.

Crossing the Rappahannock to Ferry Farm

The Olde Ferry Crossing
Watercolor on paper.

When the Washington's moved to George's boyhood home there was river ferry crossing from their plantation to a long-gone wharf on the Fredericksburg bank. The Washington's did not own or operate the ferry service which began in 1748 but, the plantation became known as Ferry Farm.

Local history explorers endeavor to create replicas of the colonial flat that went back and forth across the river but there is little specific information recorded about the small boats which were generally propelled by poles. Sometimes called bateoax, they may have been constructed in an ad lib fashion.

Washington's Women at Kenmore

WASHINGTON'S WOMEN
Acrylic on canvas created in studio from research.

The historic Kenmore Plantation house was built in the 1770s by Fielding Lewis and his wife Betty Washington Lewis. Fielding Lewis funded a large part of the Revolutionary War by lending money to Virginia and financing the Fredericksburg Gunnery (aka Gun Manufactory).

Originally called the Lewis Plantation, the estate was renamed Kenmore by the Gordon family is 1819 as homage to their ancestral home in Scotland. It's been part of the National Park Service since 1970.

This acrylic painting, Washington's

George Washington surveyed an 861-acre portion of Mr. Fielding Lewis' land on the outskirts of Fredericksburg which came to be the Kenmore Plantation. Betty Washington-Lewis and her husband Fielding Lewis lived there until they fled from the Revolutionary War with Mary Washington in 1781. Betty returned a widow. Before and after the war Martha Washington is known to have visited the two women who shared a fondness for gardening.

Women at Kenmore, was inspired by the true history of George Washington and life around Kenmore Plantation but the scene depicted by Tanya Richey is imagined.

The subjects are three very important women from George Washington's life. His sister Betty Washington Lewis, his mother Mary Ball Washington, and his wife Martha Dandridge Washington. George was Martha's second husband. Her first husband (Daniel Custis) died after only seven years of marriage.

At the time depicted in this painting, George and Mary Washington were living at Mt. Vernon, about 40 miles north of Fredericksburg.

It's well documented that Martha visited her sister-in-law (Betty Lewis) and mother-in-law (Mary Ball) regularly.

The 1,300-acre Lewis Plantation (Kenmore) was just outside the busy village of Fredericksburg connected to town by a walking path. Mary Washington's house was selected partially because it backs up very close up to the Lewis' estate.

This painting was inspired by the research for her portrait of Mary Ball Washington.

Today, the building seen in the painting still stands along with two others dating back to the late 1700s thanks to the George Washington Historic Foundation which saw fit to defend it from threats of progress on the 1920s.

COLONIAL INDEPENDENCE DAY at Ferry Farm
Watercolor on paper.

Portraits of Past and Present
Olde Fredericksburg Dock

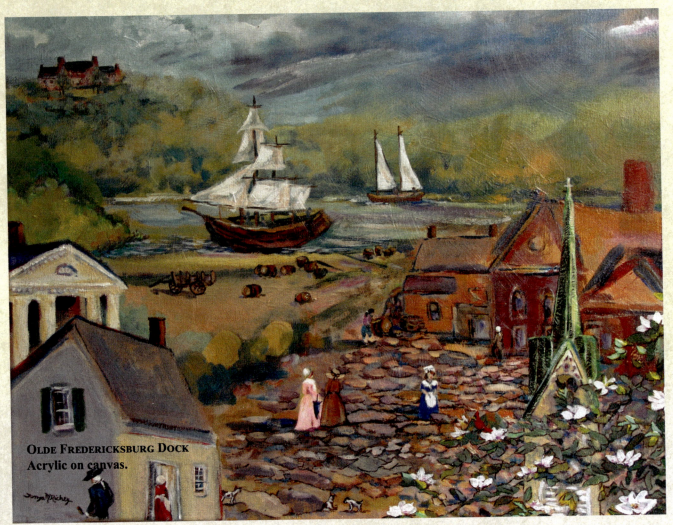

Olde Fredericksburg Dock
Acrylic on canvas.

Fredericksburg sits just below the fall line of the Rappahannock River. The village of Falmouth was the gateway between Fredericksburg and the upper river where large ships couldn't travel. Ships from England, New York, and the Caribbean came to the Fredericksburg dock regularly.

This painting, inspired by local history, is an artistic rendering envisioned by Tanya Richey and may not be historically accurate. It depicts a rolling road where tobacco barrels called hogsheads were rolled down to the docks and loaded onto the ships for far away destinations.

Olde Mill District

The west bank of the Rappahannock River was Fredericksburg's mill district processing everything from silk to sumac and pulp.

The Rappahannock River is the longest free flowing river in the Eastern United States which made for a premium shipping route. Materials came down from the mountains and foreign exchange with the Chesapeake Bay.

The river fed water powered mills and eventually provided electricity.

Inspired by a photograph Free Lance-Star newspaper, Tanya Richey used a personal technique for this painting. Broad brushstrokes loading the entire canvas with loose impressions and a secret life before painting the visible background and foreground working from the roof lines..

FREDERICKSURG HISTORIC MILLS
Acrylic on canvas.

Rising Sun Tavern

RISING SUN TAVERN
Watercolor on paper

The Rising Sun Tavern, originally named the Golden Eagle, was designed and built in 1760 by Charles Washington (George Washington's younger brother). It became a tavern in 1792. In 1907 Preservation Virginia acquired the property and restored the tavern during the 1930s. Today, it's open to the public as a museum. In the days leading up to the Revolutionary War this was a gathering place where men including Patrick Henry, Thomas Jefferson and James Monroe plotted the Revolution.

Hugh Mercer Apothecary

The Apothecary of Hugh Mercer
Watercolor on paper.

Visitors to the Hugh Mercer Apothecary will see the medical instruments and blood letting procedures of colonial life. Dr. Mercer was a well respected Scotsman who served as a surgeon in the Jacobite Army and then a general in the Continental Army. In the 1760s Fredericksburg had a thriving Scottish community.

He practiced medicine in this house from 1760-1775. His known patients included Mary Washington and eventually he purchased the Washington's Plantation at Ferry Farm.

Kenmore House

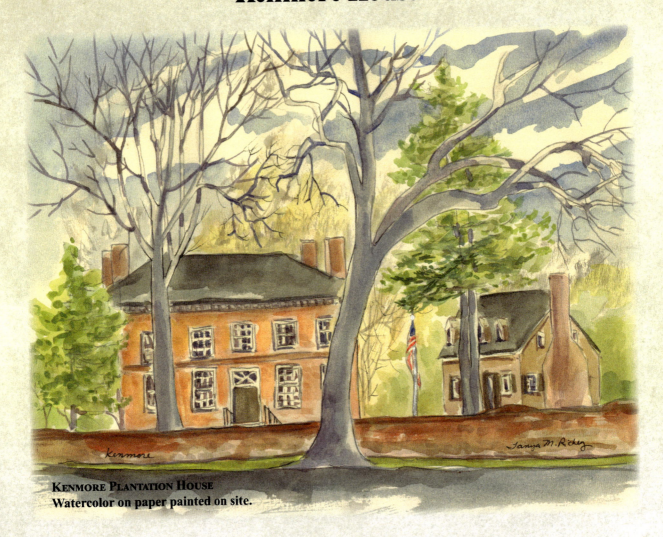

KENMORE PLANTATION HOUSE
Watercolor on paper painted on site.

Home to Fielding Lewis and his wife Betty Washington Lewis, this plantation house was once a store on a 1,300-acre plantation. Lewis, an English mercantile and American patriot, lost his fortune funding the American Revolution.

He gave supplies for ammunition including salt peter, Sulfur, gun powder, salt, flour, bacon and clothing. He also outfitted ships like *The Dragon*, a Fredericksburg built ship that protected the Rappahannock River during the Revolutionary War. His wife Betty survived him and stayed in the house until her death. For a short time it was a school. Today, the house and grounds are a museum.

Kenmore Inn

Kenmore Inn
Watercolor on paper.

This privately-owned bed and breakfast situated on Princess Anne Street is one of Fredericksburg's many historic buildings.

It was built before the Fredericksburg Fire of 1807 and survived the Civil War during which it housed Union Soldiers.

In 1931 Kenmore Inn (not to be confused with the Lewis's Kenmore plantation house) opened as a tavern and has served patrons as a restaurant, coffee shop and hotel ever since.

The Kenmore Inn currently offers guest rooms and a restaurant with a nice little bar.

Fredericksburg Fires

FREDERICKSBURG ON FIRE
Ink and oil pastel on paper

The nineteenth century was an energetic period of rapid growth. Wooden chimneys and cheap wooden structures caused three significant fires, the first was in 1799 followed by the Great Fire in 1807 during which much of Fredericksburg burnt to the ground.

The Great Fire began on the corner of Princess Anne and Lewis Streets at the Stannard House where William Stannard's body laid in wait. The kitchen may have started the blaze preparing food for his funeral.

Flames, blown up the streets by October winds, consumed the town of wooden houses leading to the abolishment of wooden chimneys in 1809.

The Wells House

"The flash of one cannon after another as they were arranged along the hills beyond, lighting up the scenery around, and the deafening shouts that followed, were sights and sounds which the novel spectator must have viewed and listened to with eager eyes and ears. It was a beautiful but awful sight."

—Mary (Mamie) Wells

During the Battle of Fredericksburg, the Wells family remained in the basement of this house while Confederate and Union forces fought outside their front door.

The house was built in 1812 for Captain Benjamin Franklin Wells on the corner of Sophia and George Street. During the Civil war the road was known as Water Street.

Confederate troops were entrenched along the city bank of the Rappahannock river as Union forces aggressed into the city. Thankfully, the Wells House survived and is now one of the few remaining buildings from the time still standing on Sophia Street.

PORTRAIT OF THE WELLS HOUSE
Watercolor on paper.

The Old Stone Warehouse

OLD STONE WAREHOUSE
Watercolor on paper sketched on site then painted in studio

The corner of William and Sophia Streets offers an optical illusion. A stone building looks single-story but the structure goes four stories down to riverside! The original building (destroyed by flood in 1807) was rebuilt by Thomas Goodwin in 1813 using coursed ashlar sandstone. Over the years this warehouse has stored tobacco and other goods before they were loaded onto ships destined for distant ports.

During the Civil War the warehouse was marred by cannon balls and used as a morgue. Since then the building has been a brewery, a feed and fertilizer storehouse, and storage for cured salt-fish.

When the new Chatham bridge (aka William Street Bridge) was built (1939-1941) Sophia Street had to be raised and the building began sliding into the river. From 1942 to the 1950s the old warehouse sat vacant until Historic Fredericksburg Foundation Inc. steped in to do the extensive work needed to stabilize it.

In 1980 Jack Edwards breathed new life into the old place when he began digging up artifacts releasing buried stories which he shared through public tours. He leased the building (co-owned by the HFFI and the City of Fredericksburg) from 1980-1986 and then again 2001-2019.

The warehouse survived the 2011 Earthquake felt from Lake Anna to north of Washington D.C., but peril struck again in 2017 when a Corps of Engineers survey study of the Chatham bridge found structural problems requiring renovation.

By 2019 plans were in place for the bridge to close for extensive repair throughout 2020. As a safety precaution the City of Fredericksburg ordered the historic warehouse vacated by October 2019. Mr. Edwards, longtime caretaker and museum advocate took as his cue and retired to Florida.

Virginia Tobacco Jar

Tobacco was a big part of Colonial Fredericksburg's economy. Many homes had a lidded tobacco jar on the fireplace mantel.

Jars, like the blue and white one in this painting, were common cannisters in farm houses and town homes as well as apothecaries where they held medical herbs. These colonial porcelain tobacco jars began as Dutch Delft porcelain with ornate designs often featuring pineapple. Of course, as America began manufacturing products knock offs evolved and became common. Colonial tobacco jars are highly collectible.

Tobacco Jar with Orange
Watercolor on paper painted in studio

This still life includes oranges as a symbol of Virginia prosperity. Shipped in from the Caribbean, perishable exotic fruits like oranges and pineapples were an expensive treat on land, especially favored in Christmastime.

Back of Old Town Hall

OLD TOWN HALL FROM MARKET SQUARE
Gauche on paper.

This richly colored painting shows the distinctive back of the old town hall viewed from Market Square. The Federal style brick building opened in 1816 after two years of construction. It housed city offices until the 1980s and is now home to the Fredericksburg Area Museum.

The ground elevation rises from the rear of the building. On Princess Anne Street it appears as two-story structure but, the lower level sandstone arches create an impressive looking building.

Market Square is a social center hosting music, festivals, and events like the French Bastille Day celebration and December Kristkringle Mart.

Princess Anne Street

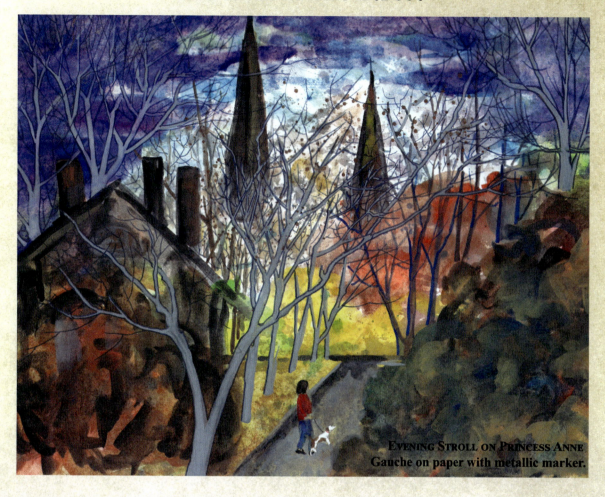

EVENING STROLL ON PRINCESS ANNE
Gauche on paper with metallic marker.

The bright colors of autumn contrasting with the dark encroaching storm clouds made the steeples look sharp and bold inspiring Richey to capture this moment on Princess Anne Street.

The building on the left is a private home and the two steeples in the background are Fredericksburg Baptist Church and St. George's Episcopal Church. Just beyond the dog walker is a glimpse of Amelia Street.

1107 Princess Anne Street was Charles Dick's house and is considered one of the oldest dwellings in Fredericksburg. The north (upper) section of Princess Anne was part of Fredericksburg's original highway (Route 1) when it ran along Princess Anne Street and Lafayette Boulevard.

Fredericksburg Square

Fredericksburg Square
Watercolor on paper

Fredericksburg Square, also known as Augustine's for a restaurant there, began as a row of townhouses in 1838. It was renovated into a mansion in 1854. Later additions by the Elks Lodge and the Post Office transformed the building into Fredericksburg's largest assembly building.

In the mid 1990s new owners purchased the property beginning a seven-year renovation creating an elegant wedding spot for locals and celebrities including Miss America 2010.

509 Caroline Street
c. 1839

Caroline Street Townhouse 509
Watercolor painted pen and ink.

Part of downtown's nineteenth century architectural history this row house on Caroline street was built between and other residential dwellings. Over time residents and businesses have changed but Caroline Street remains a vibrant stretch of Fredericksburg life. The house portrait was painted around 2014 commissioned as a housewarming gift.

The Circuit Court House

THE RENWICK BUILDING
Watercolor on paper.

This prominent building on Princess Anne Street, is often mistaken for a church but it's the Fredericksburg Corporation Courthouse, aka the Renwick Building. At the time of this painting it served as the Fredericksburg Circuit Court. When the Circuit Court moved down the street this building became home to the Fredericksburg School Board.

In 1852 Architect James Renwick was paid $300 to design a new courthouse. Townspeople protested the $14,000 cost calling it an extravagant waste.

The city counsel believed that a Renwick building would secure the town's prominence as he was well known for several buildings in Washington D.C. and New York City.

In 1829 Silas Wood donated a Paul Revere bell, which still hangs in the building's tower. 334 bells remain

> "Proud of the marks and monuments it bears to testify that its association with the country is such that her history may not be written without the name of Fredericksburg." — R. A. Kishpaugh 1912

from the Revere Foundry (known as one of the best bell makers in the United States). This is the only one in Virginia.

This building was the site of the 1768 trial of the Baptist Dissenters, workplace for James Monroe and John Marshall, and the clerk's office holds Mary Ball Washington's will

Cities & Counties,

We think of cities as big and towns as small but in Virginia there is an additional distinction between independent cities and unincorporated towns. Virginia divides into counties, areas of land containing towns. Most county population lives outside of towns so each county designates a county seat to serve as the governmental center. These unincorporated towns are part of the county they serve.

Independent cities are distinct entities- governmentally they not part of the surrounding county.

Virginia was essentially settled by venture capitalists through British Crown backed land grants and charters. Royal governors couldn't control people moving outside of the established settlements so in 1634 the predecessors of today's counties were established. The General Assembly designated eight Shires. Within the territories four settlements had been incorporated in 1618 and they retained independent status from the shires even though they were physically within the shire lines.

Counties have elected sheriffs as the key law keeper (an enduring reference to shires). Independent cities and incorporated towns have police departments.

When the shires were established, Fredericksburg was in Charles shire which extended from the Chesapeake Bay to what is now Washington D.C., down to Charlottesville, and across Richmond. Charles later separated in multiple counties including Stafford and Spotsylvania. In 1879 Fredericksburg was granted a city charter becoming an independent city- hence the Renwick courthouse building is called the "Fredericksburg Corporation Court House Building".

(Renwick buildings constructed before the Fredericksburg courthouse building include the Mark Twain House, Fifth Avenue, NYC (c. 1842; razed 1953), Grace Church, New York (1843), Smithsonian Institution Building, Washington, D.C. (1847), Calvary Church, New York (1848), Free Academy Building, City College of New York, (1849), Oak Hill Cemetery Chapel, Washington, D.C. (1850), Rhinelander Gardens, p townhouses NYC, c. 1850; razed 1956)

Irish Eyes

"Here we celebrate the bravery of all those men, in the spirit of friendship and camaraderie, and hope everyone can put aside their difference long enough to sit back and enjoy a pint, the hospitality of the establishment, and the atmosphere of people that make Fredericksburg unique."
--Irish Brigade Tavern website September 2019

Saint Patrick stands on Caroline Street every March 17th leading St. Patrick's Day celebrations and waving at passersby. *Irish Eyes* is a family run local store selling all things Irish and is connected to a heraldry and heritage center.

The Irish Brigade Tavern on Lafayette Boulevard is known for live music, but the name derives from the victors of a deadly local battle.

The Civil War pitted brother against brother in bloody battle and most Civil War history focuses on the political divides between the Northern Union and the Southern Confederacy. Fredericksburg sat between the both sides capitol cities (Washington D.C. and Richmond).

The Irish American part of that history is often left in the margins but is essential to the story of Fredericksburg.

December 13th, 1963 the Irish Brigade (a Union outfit) still battered from Antietam came head to head with the Confederate Irish of the 24th Regiment from Georgia who were entrenched behind a sturdy stone wall at Mayre's Heights.

The Irish Brigade was ordered to take the hill and break through the well defended Confederate line. The hill war already stained red and littered with the carnage of previous attacks.

The brave sons of Erin fought and died on both sides. It's said that the bold courage of the Irish Brigade was so great that the even the Confederate soldiers trying to hold the hilltop line couldn't help but cheer for their aggressor's bravery.

St. Patrick at Irish Eyes
Watercolor on paper

Olde Silk Mill

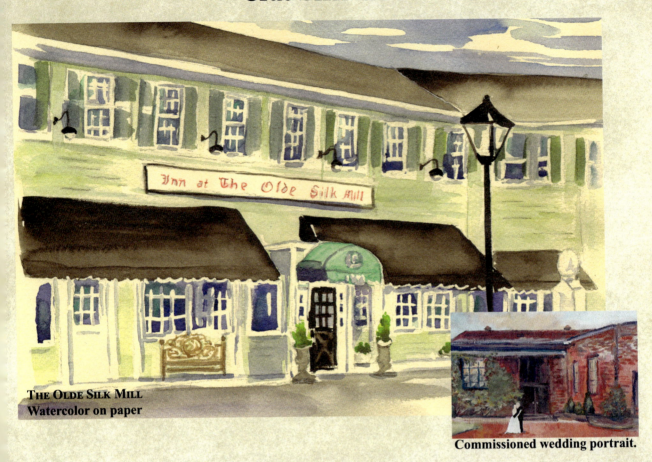

The Olde Silk Mill
Watercolor on paper

Commissioned wedding portrait.

Heading down Princess Anne Street from the Falmouth Bridge is a long building from the 1930s. It started out as the Wakefield Hotel owned by the Heflin Family. It was the third largest motor lodge on the East Coast hosting travelers from Florida to Maine

Over the years the hotel has changed names and ownership a few times but remains family run and operated. 1970-2007 it was the Fredericksburg Colonial Inn then the Whelan Family acquired the inn along with the brick silk mill building behind it (circa 1889) creating The Inn at the Olde Silk Mill. Weddings and galas celebrate special occasions in the unique atmosphere of the silk mill and guests rest comfortably in the boutique rooms.

At its height, the silk mill employed hundreds of women spinning Italian silk. The raw silk came in on ships and was spun on rail delivered machinery. Ahead of its time the silk mill was fully lit by electricity.

400 Hanover Street

The house, pictured here, was built by John J. Heflin in 1900. The stately Victorian has been private residences, the Coleman Home for Tourists (1939), Fredericksburg United Methodist Church Annex Sunday school (1855-1887) and home to former Fredericksburg mayor Tom Tomzack.

In the 1770s John Allan acquired a large parcel of land from a 2,000-acre land grant held by colonists Thomas Rayston and John Buckner. The new parcel was subdivided into eight half-acre lots called Allen Town.

Charles Yates, an English businessman, built the first house on the property. Near The Lewis Manor House (the last colonial plantation in Fredericksburg) and the what became Brooke House (Fredericksburg's first urban mansion).

Yates was the bookkeeper for a Payne, Moore & Co. grain company in Falmouth. He encouraged Fredericksburg to diversify from a tobacco town into grain, beer, wool and cotton to sustain changing economy. The shift made Fredericksburg a resilient little city ready to grow and prosper after the war continuing the spirit of progress.

In 1792 his thirteen-year-old nephew John Yates arrived from England and wrote the following:

> Fredericksburg is a very pleasant place, and we live in the best part of it, behind the main street, upon a hill looked upon as the healthiest part of the town, and where almost all of the genteel people live. The houses all have gardens and courts; the streets on the hill are nearly covered with grass, with a great many trees.
> -John Yates

St. George's Church at Night

St. George's at Night
Watercolor and ink painted on paper floated on card stock

The building, seen here, was built in 1849. Mary Ball Washington and her family attended services here in the original church building alongside other notable people in American history.

The church, always active in the Fredericksburg community, gave out food during the Great Depression and founded a boys and girls school.

St. George's is an episcopal church parish dating back to 1720. Some pewter pews remain in the building along with a few Tiffany windows.

St. George's is open most days with a busy service schedule including evening Celtic service on Sunday followed by an open Compline Service.

Compline is a bedtime prayer service carried down from Episcopal monks. The St. George's ceremony is a reflective candlelit atmosphere filled by meditative chanting.

Fredericksburg United Methodist Church

The beautiful church building on Hanover Street is home to a thriving congregation that dates back to 1800. American history is reflected in its history which includes division over slavery in 1848. Since then the church has worked to be a beacon of inclusiveness.

In 1963 is became the first contemporary Methodist church in Virginia to integrate.

The present-day building dates back to the 1880s.

Portrait of Shiloh Baptist on Sophia Street
Watercolor on paper painted on site

Shiloh Baptist Church & Walker-Grant School

"Original membership included domineering white folk, enslaved and exploited black folk, and a few free Negroes." -Shiloh Baptist Church website 2018

Shiloh Baptist Church, down by the riverside, was built in late 1830s and has been an influential congregation ever since.

Fredericksburg has a robust history from slave auction block to bustling Negro churches and businesses along Princess Anne Street. In 1890 racial division split the church creating a new beginning when the white congregation moved to a new building.

The Shiloh Baptist Church community led African-American education throughout the twentieth century. Reading lesson were taught at night during the 1920s and they published their own newspaper.

In 1905 Shiloh Baptist opened doors with the Fredericksburg Normal and Industrial Institute in the basement of the Shiloh New Site. The vocational training school was the only black school in the region offering secondary education.

In 1935 Walker-Grant School was opened across the street and in 1938 the two schools were merged becoming the first funded, public school for African Americans in Fredericksburg.

Still influential, Shiloh Baptist fill with God fearing witnesses every Sunday for Baptist gospel style worship services. Fredericksburg Public Schools continue to operate in the Walker Grant complex.

Portrait of 200 Gunnery Road. Watercolor on paper

Tea at Smythe Cottage
Fauquier Street

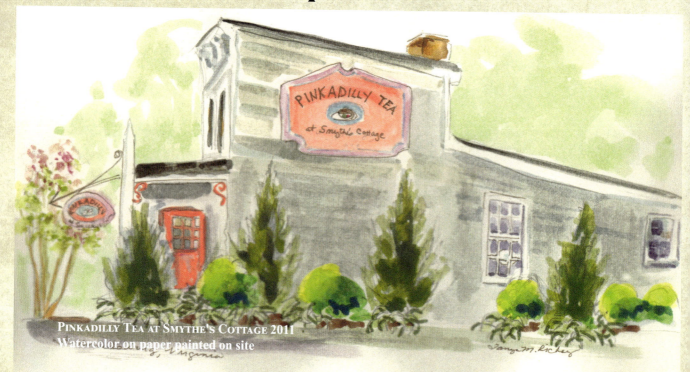

PINKADILLY TEA AT SMYTHE'S COTTAGE 2011
Watercolor on paper painted on site

Smythe's Cottage, a local landmark known for history and ghost stories, was built in the 1800s as a blacksmith's house and has been home to many restaurants and taverns over the years.

Older Fredericksburg residents remember the wooden cottage as Smythe's Cottage & Tavern serving colonial style dishes like peanut soup and roast pork.

In 2009 Kay Tipette revamped the little treasure into a brightly decorated full-service tea room serving homemade food for which she received rave reviews. The dining room was bright pink decorated with Kaye's extensive tea pot collection. In an era when coffee shops were all the rage Pinkadilly kept tea alive. (2013 the business moved to Caroline Street near the visitor center, previously The Trolley Stop sandwich shop, but the only to close in 2014.)

After Pinkadilly, Smythe's cottage was a catering BBQ business for a while then Darby O'Sullivan's Irish-American restaurant. Kristopher Scott opened Dark Star in 2019 serving "farm-to-fork" American dishes and craft cocktails.

Tru Luvs Patio
1101 Sophia Street

On the riverside of Sophia Street, a spacious restaurant featuring Rappahannock river views from the dining room and outdoor patio has enjoyed a lively history. The only other restaurant in Fredericksburg with a river view is Brock's Riverside Grill at the other end of Sophia Street near the Train Station.

2008-2013 Tru Luv's Modern American Bistro was a night life hot spot in Fredericksburg with live bands like Glass Onion and Bongo George.

Many of the patrons had enjoyed the piano bar that occupied the restaurant space before Tru Luv's and kept returning when James Cha opened his bistro. The atmosphere was lively and provided a second gallery space for Tanya Richey whose art adorned the walls.

She and many of friends were devoted patrons of Tru Luv's where she socialized and painted. Chatham sits on the hill across the river and from the bar area there is a view of downtown Fredericksburg. She used these views during work on her iconic Fredericksburg painting and was often seen working there.

After Tru Luv's closed 1101 Sophia sat vacant for several years and was purchased by local real estate developer Tommy Mitchel who secured leases from chain restaurants Uncle B's and Croaker's Spot that never opened.

The entrepreneurial spirit of downtown Fredericksburg tends to favor locally owned businesses over out of town corporations which fare better outside of town near the Spotsylvania Town Center Mall and Central Park shopping development.

Finally, in 2017 Don Mancho's Caribbean Tex Mex opened and then re-branded to Tapas Rio Riverside Latin and Italian plates.

Tru Luv's Patio 2009
Gouache on paper

Carl's Ice Cream

Carl's Ice Cream
Watercolor on paper
Painted on site.

This cash only business has been a local favorite and social center since opening in 1947. Founded by Carl Sponseller. He and his wife Margaret ran Carl's until 1972 when they sold it to two of his brothers. Carl's Frozen Custard was placed on the National Register of Historic Places in 2005.

This curbside landmark on Princess Anne Street still sells soft serve ice cream and milkshakes from original Electro Freeze machines. Open February to November, rain shine there is always a line of friendly people waiting for their tasty treat undeterred by bad weather or lack of seating.

Castiglia's on William Street

Castiglia's at Night
Mixed Medium

Even before Castilglia's built a rooftop bar it was an energetic place. Locally owned and operated by the Castiglia family Luigi featuring his mother's authentic recipes from Naples, Italy.

A patron of arts and brilliant businessman, Luigi allows area artists to display bold artwork throughout the restaurant and bar. After this painging Casiglia's renovated upward with a rooftop area of live music.

This stretch of William Street is popular with neighboring Vivify Burger and Lounge (opened 2013) and La Petite Auberge (family run French cuisine sine 1981).

Art Comes Alive

"A rich man without charity is a rogue; and perhaps it would be no difficult matter to prove that he is also a fool."

—Henry Fielding

Art Comes Alive was a September gala featuring invited artist for a unique fundraising event. 2011-2014 Tanya Richey was delighted to support for the Fredericksburg Area Museum by painting live. Participating artists created original works of art right before guests' eyes. At the end of the four-hour event the art was auctioned off to support the museum fetching thousands of dollars.

Painting in public offers unique challenges but Richey thrived at the opportunity for onlookers see the evolution of a painting. Although most of the invited artists arrived with paintings already in progress she took it as a challenge giving donors the full experience of watching from first paint to last brush stroke.

Each artist was provided a small spotlight illuminating their workspace in the dim evening ambiance of the museum. At that time The Fredericksburg Regional Area Museum was located in the old Planters National Bank building (c.

1927) and former Carly retail shop (c. 1800s). The two properties had been combined in the McKann Center in 2006

In 2016 The Fredericksburg Area Museum and Cultural Center (there since 2008) auctioned the building and relocated the museum to the other side of William Street.

The painting *Impressions of Caroline Street* depicts a stretch of Caroline

Street with many popular shops and establishments including Sorry Mom Tattoo.

At the time this painting was created the Tanya Richey Gallery occupied 817 Caroline Street. (Two doors down from the restaurant Soup & Taco Etc.)

Caroline street has been a bustling stretch of Fredericksburg's commerce from the beginning. Today, the street is mainly small local businesses including art cooperatives and galleries. Art First, Brush Strokes, Pon Shop and local artist painted out in the streets during this era in annual events like Art Attack, Via Colori, and monthly First Fridays.

Art is such an important part of Fredericksburg culture that the city created the Fredericksburg Arts and Cultural District. All businesses in the arts district may apply for city incentives just by showcasing art.

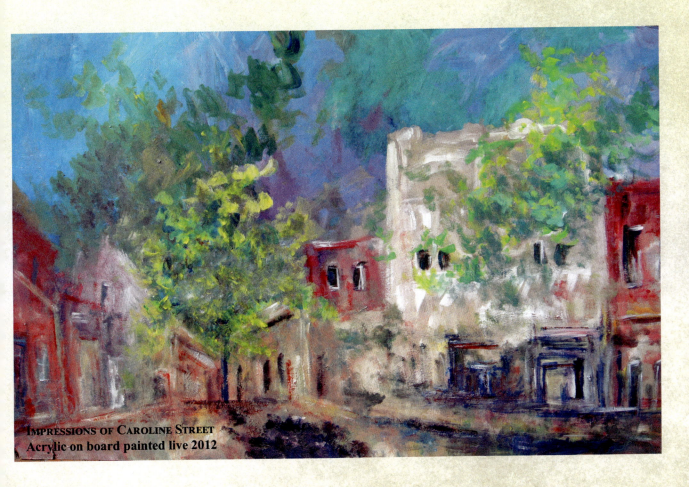

IMPRESSIONS OF CAROLINE STREET
Acrylic on board painted live 2012

Gari Melchers Belmont

OUTBUILDINGS AT BELMONT
Acrylic on canvas painted plein aire

Across the Rappahannock River in Stafford, just north of Falmouth, a grand Georgian Mansion with out buildings and gardens supports the intersection of history and art.

Famous for portraits and impressionistic painting Belmont was his home and studio from 1916-1932.

The Estate's house is circa 1970s with a stone studio build in 1920.

Belmont is an exemplary hub of local culture with creative programs, educational opportunities and community partnerships.

The Stafford County Visitors Center in on location and cooperative efforts with local clubs and organizations are routine.

Local Master Gardeners and Master Naturalist help maintain the restored gardens and nature trails. Local clubs like the Mary Ball Womans Club contribute to the upkeep and restorative efforts of th buildings and the property is managed by University of Mary Washington Museums.

Theatre and the Arts

Fredericksburg is more than industry and battlefields. Creative arts thrive in our little city.

Riverside Theatre brings in professional talent like Sally Struthers and the Fredericksburg Center for the Creative Arts (FCCA) is a world class art gallery and a partner of the Virginia Museum of Fine Arts. Even the local schools have award winning drama departments and bands

Stage Door Productions community theater group holds one-act play competitions, presents well known stage plays, and includes local children through Kids on Stage.

It takes a fleet of volunteers behind stage front actors in every show and Fredericksburg's theatrical community

2012-2016 Tanya Richey contributed to the lively theatrical community capturing scenes from Stage Door performances. Proceeds from these works of art benefited the performance community as part of her campaign to give back to the community.

"As an artist I'm not always able to make cash donations but through my art I can always find a way to give back."
— Tanya Richey

GIRLS OF THE GOLDEN AFTERNOON
Watercolor on paper
Painted during Kid's on Stage performance of Alice in Wonderland.

Fredericksburg
Gateway to the World

Modern Dinner Boat in Spring, 2014
Watercolor on paper

Early America saw the commercial benefit of local river access to the Chesapeake Bay and Atlantic Ocean. The same trade routes along life baring waters had nourished the native people.

The Rappahannock River's named derives from indigenous peoples phrase for fast rising river water. Early German pioneers forged inland through the thick forest, but English settlers saw the waterway as the key to prosperity. Timber, crops, and even gold from further inland needed to escape Virginia to have value and the local rivers were perfect. Eventually, canals were built to expand the water routes into County but the investment ended up an expensive boondoggle as river ways were replaced by railways.

Roads improved and highways evolved bringing Route 1 and eventually I-95 through town connecting the East Coast from Maine to Florida and Routes 3 and 17 reaching west.

As interstate travel improved Fredericksburg's international trade wained but the spirit seeded by the worldwide port which had birthed factories, and prepared the city for the industrial era remains present today through the numerous city partnerships including France, Germany, Nepal, Italy, and Ghana.

ANTIQUE CAR SHOW ON CAROLINE STREET
Watercolor on paper.

Riverboat on the Rappahannock

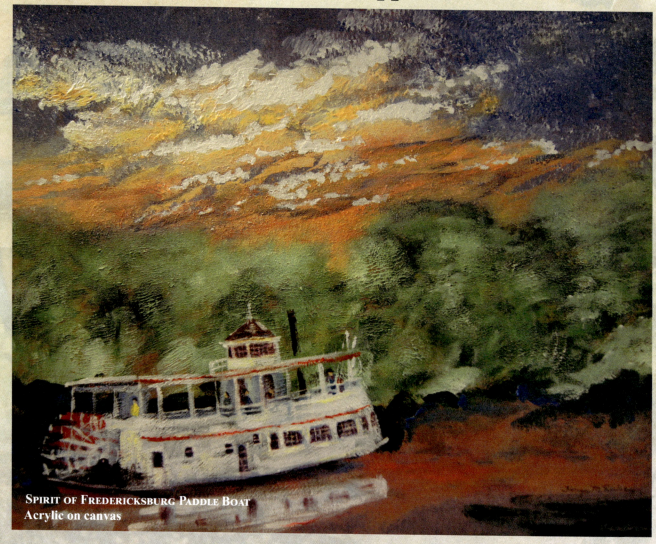

SPIRIT OF FREDERICKSBURG PADDLE BOAT
Acrylic on canvas

Paddle boats are often depicted on the Mississippi River but they used to navigate the Rappahannock River as well. The boat shown in this painting provided dinner cruises during the summer from the Fredericksburg docks until 2016 when the Fredericksburg area of the river had become so silted in that the paddles were not longer able to navigate to the city docks safely.

Rivers used to be the main transportation lines in Virginia, roads were difficult to travel but boats of all types and sizes came to port in Fredericksburg.

Construction of the Embrey Dam, the rise of the railroad and other factors led to a decline in river shipping but the river is still popular for recreation boas like canoes and kayaks.

Modern boat travel is still a big part of the summer river-scape.

The 19th century brought steamboats to passenger travel. By that time Fredericksburg port business was all but shut down. The building of dams lowered the water levels significantly limiting the port. Baltimore and New York had become the popular transatlantic ports with service to prominent Philadelphia.

In 1817 Captain Charles Weems started a passenger steam boat company with service Chesapeake's Western Shore and Baltimore and kept a practical monopoly on Virginia riverboat travel for 88 years running out of Baltimore and along the Patuxent, Potomac and Rappahannock rivers.

A regular schedule connecting Fredericksburg to Baltimore and Norfolk offered affordable and comfortable service.

In 1828 The Weems Steamboat Company's new side paddle boat, the Patuxent, began a route connecting Fredericksburg to Baltimore off the lower Patuxent River navigating the Rappahannock River to Fredericksburg but the line was short lived and by 1830 Weems Rappahannock route was gone. Consistent passenger travel resumed in 1856 with a new company named the Fredericksburg Line (operated by Jacob Tome and Mason L. Weems). *The Richmond* took passengers between Fredericksburg and Baltimore until 1901 when it burned at the Fredericksburg dock.

Then, came the trains.

The run from Baltimore to Fredericksburg provided transportation for young people going to school in Fredericksburg, Richmond and Williamsburg. In the first quarter of this century, Fredericksburg Normal School offered two years of high school work as well as two years of college.

—Louis E. Gray

Behind the Train Station

Trains began arriving in Fredericksburg during January of 1837. The passenger depot was located where the checkered Purina tower stands today. The current station location opened in 1910 with a complex of brick buildings that took up most of block

Rail transport was popular with both passengers and freight. In earlier times passengers arriving by ship transferred to rail service.

In addition to milling, Fredericksburg has had several prosperous factory businesses producing all sort of thing thanks to the rail line which eventually replaced river transports in and out of Fredericksburg.

A pants factory, an ice factory, and cellophane factory have all been major employers in Fredericksburg. The old cellophane factory is now home to Bowman's Distillery which was the first whiskey company in Virginia to be legal after prohibition.

Today, the train is a popular way for people to commute to Washington D.C.

Amtrak service runs through Fredericksburg on a limited schedule but the VRE (Virginia Rail Express) began service in 1992 offering commuter service into D.C. in the morning and back to Fredericksburg in the evening giving locals a great way to avoid I-95 traffic.

The checkered building, the Purina tower, was a grain tower for The Young-Sweetser Co. in 1919.

Another interesting bit of history in this section of town is the old gasification plant. Fredericksburg streetlights and homes were illuminated by gas from the gas plant from 1900 until WWII. Effort to modernize and switch to a propane facility ended in an explosion which evacuated about 12 blocks and closed the plant leaving a burnt-out shell before it was eventually converted to offices.

PURINA TOWER AND TRAIN WAREHOUSES
Watercolor on paper.

Pufferbellies

TRAIN BRIDGE PUFFER-BELLIES
Watercolor on paper en plein air

"See the little puffer bellies all in a row" is the beginning of a children's folk song.

Puffer-belly is a common nickname for steam engine trains but in this painting it refers to the little birds sitting in a row at the Fredericksburg docks with their bellies puffed out to keep warm.

This watercolor captures the Fredericksburg train bridge during the last days of autumn just before the colorful leaves are gone and things begin to frost.

The William Street Bridge

COMMUTERS' VIEW ON CHATHAM BRIDGE
Mixed medium on canvas board

A commuter's view in winter driving into town across the Chatham Bridge onto William Street. Working in her Fredericksburg Gallery Richey traveled across this bridge daily and enjoyed the dramatic winter scene captured with acrylic on canvas.

There has been a bridge crossing in this location since the 1800s. An earlier bridge called "Scott's Bridge" was destroyed during the Civil War.

After the war an iron toll bridge was erected but it was washed away by flooding in the early 1900s. Today's bridge was put into service around 1937.

Dogs of Fredericksburg

Fredericksburg may be one of the most dog friendly towns in America.

Fredericksburg is home to Annie, Virginia's first official canine clerk. The black Labrador was officially sworn in November 17th, 2014 with duties including raising office moral.

Downtown dog walkers are greeted by public water bowls outside many shops and restaurants.

Fredericksburg has been a canine center since 1698 when local tribes and settlers began trading at the yearly Dog Mart. Manahoac, Algonquin, Pawmonkey and other tribes traded produce and pelts for English hunting dogs.

In 1619 the Virginia Assembly forbade the sale of dogs but in 1677 established the marte or fair as a legal place to sell and trade English dogs and the annual event continued until the Revolutionary War.

Dogs Welcome inside

1927 the event was revived with the Dog Curb Market at City Park and grew dramatically. A 1937 article in Time Magazine drew 7,000 people and 641 dogs to the 1938 event. After WWII, in the 1950s, the event drew even more acclaim when it was featured in National Geographic imagine bringing over 12,000 people to Caroline Street.

The location of the regional Often held in Spotsylvania Country it has been a Fredericksburg Chamber of Commerce event overseen by the Izaak Walton League since 1948. The modern focus is on promoting dog adoption.

In addition to dog friendly trick-or-treating at Halloween, pet photo's with Santa the Jack Russel Dog Show is held at the Expo Center.

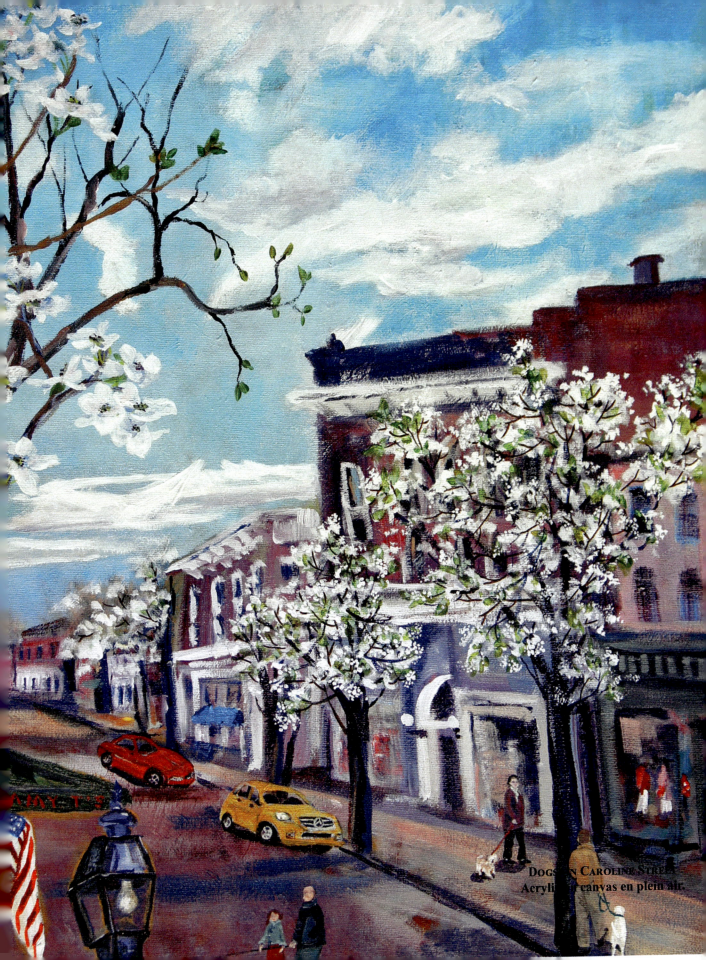

Dogs on Caroline Street
Acrylic on canvas en plein air.

The Chicken Controversy

Rooster and Hen House
Water color on paper

Chickens have always been common in traditional Virginia life. Roosters stands proudly in front of wooden hen houses as seen here.

This gauche watercolor painting uses several techniques including resist and washes.

In the past it was not uncommon for homes and restaurants to have chickens and roosters on the property, but contemporary public health concerns pushed the chicken out of most American towns and onto rural farms.

Today, however, backyard chickens are making a comeback as more Americans have renewed interest in fresh eggs and poultry companions.

There's now lively debate in Fredericksburg and other towns as chicken advocates push local governments to overturn poultry bans in populated areas and bring back the backyard chicken.

Around 2012 the Fredericksburg City Council began changing local laws to permit chickens within the city limits of Fredericksburg.

Non-commercial, licensed chickens for home use eggs are allowed as long as they are kept in clean, fenced, covered enclosure away from the main house and neighbors property lines.

Annual city chicken license in 2018 was $10 (the same as a bee license) but roosters are still banned.

Inspired by the Rubaiyat of Omar Khayyam., one of Artist Tanya Richey's favorite books.
Mixed medium on watercolor paper using watercolor, oil pastel crayons, and metallic markers.

Animals and Agriculture
The Fredericksburg Fair

FREDERICKSBURG FAIR WITH NOJOE THE CLOWN
Acrylic on canvas

The Fredericksburg Fair claims to be the oldest agricultural fair in the United States. The original fair was established by the Virginia House of Burgess in 1738 "for the sale of cattle, provisions, goods, wares, and all kinds of merchandise".

In addition to traditional livestock trading, awarding ribbons for things like the biggest cucumber and best fruit jam, the annual fair hosts popular events like demolition derby, mud bogs, and monster truck shows. Each night offers different entertainment including carnival games and rides, and the crowning of Miss Fredericksburg. In the 1960s the then unknown singer Tammy Wynette gave a performance.

Virginia Cows

Cow Lick Creek
Watercolor on paper

Raising cattle is important to rural Virginia. Virginians eat beef, tan the hide for leather, drink milk and in earlier times used the fat for candle making.

In Virginia only dairy cows are kept in barns and even the dairy cows are sent out into the pasture during the day.

Licking water from the country streams, cows are as common as churches in the Virginia countryside.

To keep entertained during long car rides into town there is a game of counting cows. The object is to count the most cows on the way to your destination but watch out for graveyards and cemeteries which, according the game rules, kill your cows. After passing a graveyard, players pray to spy a church so that their cow count is returned.

Summer Barn

JOANNIE'S BARN
Watercolor on paper

A summer view of country hay barn as the fields are growing tall with hay before it's bush hogged.

Today, mechanical and even GPS automated balers are used creating the huge stacks of hay which sits in the field but in the past the hay was baled by hand into movable bundles secured with twine which were stored in the barn's loft.

Many barn and field fires were caused by hay bales lighting on fire. If the hay is not dry when it's gathered up the bales are prone to spontaneous combustion.

In Virginia, hay (cut grass) is primarily used to feed horses and cows.

Weathervane Barn

WEATHERVANE BARN
Oil pastel on paper

View of a local barn looking out of a farmhouse window. Barns were generally built close enough to the house to keep watch. The roofs of many barns in the area were made of metal and have turned orange with rust over the years.

Slowly, these barns are disappearing as they fall into disrepair and farming becomes less common. As they are torn down the barn wood is often collected and reused as flooring or home decor accents.

Virginia Wild Turkey

VIRGINIA WILD TURKEY
Oil pastel on paper.

Wild American Turkey have been found in Virginia since European settlers arrived. Presumable they were common to native locals long before that. They were an important food source during colonial times but were hunted into rarity.

In 1912 Virginia passed the Robin Bill, a law that prohibited the sale of wild turkey in markets and in 1922 Virginia began breeding and farming programs to restore the wild turkey population.

Wild American turkeys are still found in area forests and can be hunted during the fall hunting season.

Wild Life

The Rappahannock River starts in the Blue Ridge mountains and flows from Chester Gap past Fredericksburg flowing all the way to the Chesapeake Bay a mere 20 miles from the mouth of the Potomac. It cuts through forested land through the Piedmont to the fall line at Fredericksburg and then into brackish water through Virginia's coastal plain.

Local ecology is a rich meeting point where inland creatures like fox and butterfly live beneath seagulls and the rivers provide trout, shad, and crab.

Traveling west from Fredericksburg toward the mountains you come into the foothills of the Blue Ridge Mountains. There is a long history of solitary people settling into isolated cabins in the valleys and on the hillsides.

This painting depicts a more rural way of life up-river above the fall line where the terrain rises creating the Piedmont.

The indigenousness people were hunter gatherers living off the local ecosystem. Western settlers cleared large areas of forest developing farmland and harvesting timber.

The Rockey Fall Line
Watercolor on paper

Rappahannock Winter

Winter Wilderness
Warercolor on paper.

Travel any direction but north from Fredericksburg and you will fine wilderness.

You don't have to go very far off the main road to find snowy wooded scenes like this anywhere around Fredericksburg.

This painting is watercolor painted wet on dry watercolor paper. The snow and tree bark effects are created by scratching the paint off to reveal the paper beneath after the watercolor has dried.

Afterword

Tanya Richey was an International fine artist painting locally.

Fredericksburg held a special place in Tanya's heart. Born in Virginia (Hungry Mother State Park in Marion) but she said she was raised across America.

During her childhood Tanya was never in one spot long enough to put down roots but after getting married in the 1960s she and her husband settled in Northern Virginia and she anchored herself. Over the next forty years she would come to consider the Rappahannock area her home no matter where in the world she lived.

As an amateur artist her first blue ribbon was won at the Fredericksburg Art Show. From there her mastery of fine art blossomed and she became an internationally collected, self sustaining, fine artist. After years showing in galleries like the Watergate in Alexandria, VA The Penta Hotel in Heidelberg, Germany and Middle Street Gallery in Washington, Virginia she moved her home based studio to Little Washington were she opened Tanya M. Richey Windflower Studio Gallery, the first single artist gallery in Rappahannock County. In 2010, after a stint in Columbia SC, and Wilmington NC, she moved to Stafford County, VA and opened her sixth successful art gallery at 817 Caroline Street.

Resources

The stories in this book are distilled from years of research, local interviews, observations, and yarns shared by friends and patrons. The following is an abbreviated list of resources useful getting to know Fredericksburg.

Rappahannock Regional Library Library Point
https://www.librarypoint.org/blogs/post/mill-sites-and-water-power/

University of Mary Washington Library
http://resources.umwhisp.org/Fredericksburg/plats.htm

National Park Service • Chesapeake Bay Office
https://home.nps.gov/cajo/planyourvisit/upload/06_Rappahannock.pdf

City of Fredericksburg Historic District Handbook
https://www.fredericksburgva.gov/DocumentCenter/View/175/Historic-District-Handbook?bidId=

Historic Foundation Fredericksburg, Inc. https://hffi.org/

Central Rappahannock Heritage Center https://www.crhcarchives.org/

Patawomeck Heritage Foundation http://www.patawomeckindians.org

Virginia Department of Education
http://www.doe.virginia.gov/instruction/history/virginias-first-people/today/patawomeck/index.shtml

The George Washigton Foundation http://www.kenmore.org/

Calvert Marine Museum. P. 0. Box 97, Solomons, Maryland 20688
Bugeye Times, Vol. 70 No. 4. winter 1983 "A Short History: The ' Steamboat Line".

"EARLY STEAMBOAT TRAVEL FONDLY REMEMBERED" by LOUISE E. GRAY
Daily Press/The Times-Herald April 3, 1991

"Historic Fredericksburg The Story of an Old Town" By John T. Goolrick. 1922
http://www.gutenberg.org/files/39403/39403-h/39403-h.htm

History of Fredericksburg Virginia by Alvin T. Embrey

Index

Apothecary	10, 25, 31	Young-Swwtser Co.	59
African-American	45	Payne, Moore & Co.	41
Baptist Dissenter Trial	37		
Battle of Fredericksburg	2-	**Fire**	27, 31, 38, 68
Blacksmith	36	**Gasification**	59
Blue Heron	13	**General assembly**	37
Bridges		**German/Germany**	12, 54, 55, 73, 79
Chatham Bridge	10, 15, 30, 61	**Hogshead**	22
Falmouth Bridge	13, 40	**Industrial**	13, 43, 55
Scott's Bridge	10, 61	**Irish**	
Train bridge	10, 60	Sons of Erin	38
William Street Bridge	30, 60	Irish Brigade	38
Churches		24thRegiment	38
Presbyterian Church	9	**Jacobite Army**	25
St. Georges Episcopal	9, 33, 42, 45	**Mills**	10, 23, 40, 58
Shiloh Baptist Church		Beer	41, 30
Civil War	8, 10, 27, 29, 30, 38, 61	Cotton	41
City Hall/Town Hall	32	Fertilizer	30
Colonial Era	40, 42	Grain	41, 59
Colonial Inn	40, 42	Grist	10
Compline service	42	Pulp	23
Confederate soldiers	38	Salt peter	26
Continental Army	25	Saltfish	31
Corps of Engineers	31	Silk	10, 23, 40
Dam, Embrey	10, 13, 56, 57	Sumac	10, 23
Dogs	63	Tobacco	18, 22, 30, 31 41
Dutch Delft	31	Wool	41, 10
Electricity	40, 23	**Motor lodge**	40
Education	52, 45	**Mountains**, Blue Ridge	23, 72
England/ English	13, 16, 11, 22, 26, 42, 55	**National Park Service**	18, 20
		Native Indians	8, 12, 13
Factories		Patawomeck	12, 13
Ice factory	58	Algonquian	12, 62
Cellophane factory	58	Manahoac	12, 62
Bowman's distillery	58	Pawmonkey	62
Purina Tower	56		
Pants	59	**People**	
VRE	59	Annie	62

Augustine Washington	16, 34
Benjamin Franklin Wells	29
Betty Washington Lewis	20, 21, 26
Bongo George	47
Carl Sponseller	48
Charles Dick	33
Charles Weems	57
Charles Yates	41
Daniel Custis	21
Fielding Lewis	20, 21, 26
Gari Melcher	52
George Eskridge	16
George Mason	17
George Washington	15-19
Gordon family	20
Hugh Mercer	4, 25
Jack Edwards	31
Jacob Tome	57
James Monroe	24, 37
James Renwick	5, 36
John Allan	41
John Buckner	4, 41
John J. Heflin	20, 40
John Marshall	37
John Smith	4, 12, 13
John Yates	41
Kay Tipette	46
Luigi Castiglia	40
Madon L. Weems	57
Marquis de Lafayette	17
Martha Dandridge Washington	21
Mary Ball Washington	15-17, 21, 37, 46, 52
Mary Mamie Wells	29
Patrick Henry	24
Pocahontas	13
Sally Struthers	53
Silas Wood	36
Tammy Wynette	66
Thomas Goodwin	30
Thomas Jefferson	24
Thomas Rayston	41
Tom Tomzack	41
William Stannard	28
Wayne Newton	13
William Wallace Tooker	13
William Ball	16

Local Places

Arts and cultural district	15
Belmont	52
Boys and Girls School	42
Brooke House	41
Carl's Frozen Custard	48
Carly retail shop	50
Cherry Point	16
Corperation Court House	36-37
county seat	37
Circuit Court	36
Elks lodge	34
FCCA	53
Ferry Farm	16, 19, 21, 25
Fredericksburg Area Museum	32, 50
Fredericksburg Square	34
Gunnery	20, 45
Kenmore Inn	27
Kenmore Plantation House	21, 26-27
Lewis Plantation	20-21
Marye's Heights	38
Market Square	32
McKann Center	50
Meditation Rock	15
Morgue	30
Mt. Vernon	21
Normal and Industrial Institute	44
Pinkadilly	46
Planters National Bank	50
Popes Creek	16, 18
Post Office	34
Rising Sun Tavern	10, 24
Row houses	34-35
Shiloh Baptist Church	44-45
Smythe Cottage	46
Soup ad Taco etc.	51

Warehouse	30-31, 50		
Wakefield Hotel	40	**Towns and Counties**	
Walker-Grant School	45	Baltimore	57
		Charles shire	37
Paul Revere Bell	36-37	Charlottesville	37
Poultry	64, 67	Chesapeake Bay	29, 37, 54, 71
Revolutionary War	18, 10-13, 16, 18-19, 20-24, 26, 56-57, 71	Chester Gap	71
		Epping Forest	16
		Falmouth	8, 10, 13, 22, 40, 41, 52
Rivers			
Rappahannock River	54, 57	Lake Anna	31
Potomac River	12-13, 16 18, 57, 71	Lancaster Va.	15
Fall line	12, 22, 72	New York	22, 36-37, 57
Patuxent river	57	Northern Neck	16
The Robin Bill	70	Philadelphia	57
Rolling road	22	Stafford	11, 13, 18, 37, 52
Royston-Buckner Plan	8	Spotsylvania	12, 37, 47, 62
Scotland/ Scottish	20, 25	Washington D.C.	31, 36-38, 58-59
Shad	11, 13, 71	**Trains**	10, 47, 57-59, 60
Sheriff	37	**Union soldiers**	27, 29, 38
Ships		**House of Burgess**	8, 66
The Dragon	26	**West Indies**	11
Flat boats	19		
Ferry	19		
Schooners	11		
Shipping routes	18, 23, 57		
Canals	55		
Waterways	18, 55		
Spain/Spanish	11		
Streets			
Amelia Street	33		
Caroline Street	3, 9, 15, 35, 38, 56, 50-51, 62.		
Charles Street	15		
Lewis Street	17, 28		
Fauquier Street	46		
Lafayette Blvd	33, 38		
Princess Anne Street	27, 32-33, 36, 40, 45, 48		
Sophia Street	15, 29, 30, 47		
Water Street *see Sopia Street*			
William Street	28, 30, 40, 49, 50, 61		

About the Author

TANYA RICHEY, ARTIST WITH MARY JOLLY, AN ORIGINAL PATRON Fredericksburg Wine Festival.

Tanya Richey enjoyed painting and traveling throughout America, Mexico, Europe, Soviet Russia, Egypt, China, and Japan and enjoyed meeting new cultures. In 2013 she returned to Baden-Wurttemberg for the first time in almost 25 years.

She'd lived in the Heidelberg area as an ex-patriot during the 1980s, the same time she was transitioning from emerging artist to professional artist. During that time she embraced the spirit of a modern-day itinerant painter manifesting impressions of her experiences with her paint brush.

In 2018 Tanya Richey passed away after a yearlong battle with cancer. Many of the moments she'd captured were already part of the past but these captured moments, the Spirit of Fredericksburg as she knew it, remains in public and private collections around the world as her contribution to preservation.

stunning impressions of the Spirit of Fredericksburg.

Made in the USA
Lexington, KY
11 December 2019